World Book's Learning Ladders

Rain Forest Animals

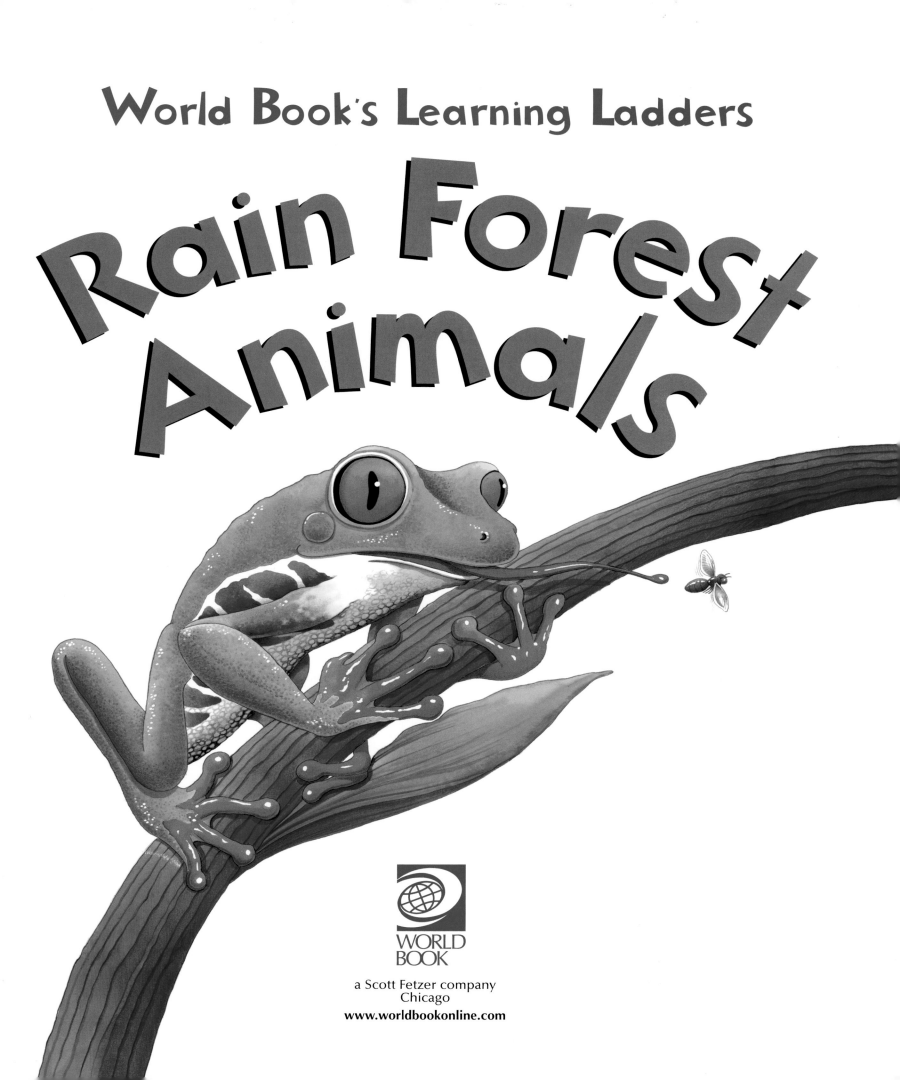

WORLD BOOK

a Scott Fetzer company
Chicago
www.worldbookonline.com

World Book, Inc.
180 North LaSalle Street
Suite 900
Chicago, Illinois 60601
USA

For information about other World Book publications, visit our website at www.worldbook.com or call 1-800-WORLDBK (967-5325).

For information about sales to schools and libraries, call 1-800-975-3250 (United States); 1-800-837-5365 (Canada).

2008 revised printing

Library of Congress Cataloging-in-Publication Data

Rain forest animals.
    p. cm. -- (World Book's learning ladders)
  Summary: "Introduction to animals that live in the rain forest using simple text, question and answer format, illustrations, and photos. Features include puzzles and games, fun facts, a resource list, and an index"--Provided by publisher.
  Includes bibliographical references and index.
  ISBN 978-0-7166-7729-1
  1. Rain forest animals--Juvenile literature.
I. World Book, Inc.
QL112.R35 2007
591.734--dc22
                2007018911

World Book's Learning Ladders
ISBN 978-0-7166-7725-3 (set, hc.)

Also available as:
ISBN 978-0-7166-7760-4 (e-book, Learning Hub)
ISBN 978-0-7166-7761-1 (e-book, Spindle)
ISBN 978-0-7166-7762-8 (e-book, EPUB3)
ISBN 978-0-7166-7763-5 (e-book, PDF)

Printed in China by Shenzhen Wing King Tong Paper Products Co, Ltd., Shenzhen, Guangdong
10th printing February 2017

Staff

Executive Committee
President: Jim O'Rourke
Vice President and Editor in Chief: Paul A. Kobasa
Vice President, Finance: Donald D. Keller
Vice President, Marketing: Jean Lin
Vice President, International Sales: Maksim Rutenberg
Director, Human Resources: Bev Ecker

Editorial
Director, Digital & Print Content Development: Emily Kline
Editor, Digital & Print Content Development: Kendra Muntz
Senior Editor: Shawn Brennan
Senior Editor: Dawn Krajcik
Manager, Indexing Services: David Pofelski
Manager, Contracts & Compliance (Rights & Permissions):
  Loranne K. Shields

Digital
Director, Digital Product Development: Erika Meller

Graphics and Design
Senior Art Director: Tom Evans
Coordinator, Design Development and Production: Brenda B. Tropinski

Manufacturing/Pre-Press
Production/Technology Manager: Anne Fritzinger
Proofreader: Nathalie Strassheim

This edition is an adaptation of the Ladders series published originally by T&N Children's Publishing, Inc., of Minnetonka, Minnesota.

Photographic credits: Cover: © age fotostock/SuperStock; p4: Planet Earth Pictures; p6: Bruce Coleman Ltd; p7: Oxford Scientific Films; p8: Tony Stone Images; p9: Bruce Coleman Ltd; p11: Planet Earth Pictures; p14: Oxford Scientific Films; p15: Bruce Coleman Ltd; p16: Oxford Scientific Films; p17: Bruce Coleman Ltd; p18: Oxford Scientific Films; p21: Bruce Coleman Ltd; p22: Oxford Scientific Films.

Illustrators: Steve Holmes, Jon Stuart

What's inside?

This book tells you about lots of exciting animals that live in the hot and steamy rain forests of South America. Some of the animals swing or fly through the trees and others roam the forest floor.

Monkey

Monkeys live in groups in the trees. They are amazing acrobats that leap from branch to branch and swing from the dangling vines. When monkeys play, they screech and whoop loudly. What a racket!

A monkey holds onto the branches with its strong **arms**.

Monkeys **chat** and squabble with each other. They also make funny faces.

A golden lion tamarin monkey has a shaggy, golden coat. The fur around its face is so thick, you can't see its ears!

It's a fact!

Howler monkeys are the noisiest animals in the rain forest. You can hear their deafening howls miles away!

Good **eyes** help a monkey spot danger and stay safe.

To keep steady, a monkey curls its long **tail** tightly around a branch.

Monkeys have **thumbs**. Like yours, they are useful for grasping things.

 # Sloth

A sloth hooks its **claws** tightly over a branch, so that it doesn't fall.

A sloth spends most of its life hanging upside down, fast asleep. When this strange-looking creature wakes up, it slowly crawls along its branch, looking for leaves to eat. About once a week, it creeps down the tree trunk to the ground.

A sloth crawls along the forest floor. It takes half an hour to move as far as you can walk in one minute!

Shaggy **hair** grows down from a sloth's body. This helps rain to run off easily.

A **baby sloth** clings to its mother's belly, where it is cozy and safe.

A sloth hardly ever washes! Green **slime** grows on its hair.

A sloth sleeps for up to 18 hours a day. It doesn't need to eat much food because it is hardly ever awake.

 # Bat

When night falls, bats wake up. They stretch their wings and leave their daytime resting places in trees and caves. Bats have excellent ears and eyes to help them find their way around in the dark.

A bat's hands are its **wings**. Its fingers support a smooth, stretchy skin.

Bats go to sleep hanging upside down. They fold their leathery wings across their furry bodies to stay warm.

A bat has a **furry body**. It is the only animal with fur that can fly.

This bat's large **ears** pick up sounds that even you cannot hear.

These baby tent bats snuggle up in a palm leaf. They will stay here until they are big enough to fly away.

A big **nose** sniffs out the ripest fruit and tastiest insects to eat.

Colorful birds

High up in the leafy trees, rainbow-colored birds sing and squawk. They swoop and climb through the trees looking for berries and nuts. You may even spot a macaw, one of the biggest birds in the rain forest, munching a tasty treat.

Colorful **markings** help macaws spot each other among the leaves.

It's a fact!

Hummingbirds are the smallest birds in the world. One kind is so tiny that it can perch on the end of a pencil!

A macaw's waterproof **feathers** act like a raincoat. They keep out the pouring rain.

A strong, hooked **beak** is perfect for cracking open tough nuts to eat.

Sharp, curly claws, called **talons**, help a macaw grip branches or hold nuts.

A toucan's giant beak looks heavy, but it is hollow and light. It's made from the same material as your fingernails.

In the trees

The trees are packed with noisy animals playing and looking for food. Look how they leap, climb, and fly!

How many tiny hummingbirds are flying around the flowers?

12

Words you know

Here are words that you read earlier in this book. Say them out loud, then find the things in the picture.

beak   **claws**   **thumbs**
wings   **tail**   **feathers**

 # Frog

A frog breathes through its **slimy skin**, as well as through its nose.

All kinds of brightly colored frogs leap around the steamy forest floor. They splash in rivers and make their homes in puddles left by the rain. The red-eyed tree frog in the big picture is an expert at climbing trees.

Strong back **legs** are useful for hopping after insects or springing away from enemies.

Two poison-arrow frogs crouch on a leaf. Their bright patterns warn hungry enemies that they are deadly poisonous.

Huge **bulging eyes** quickly spot tiny insects buzzing past.

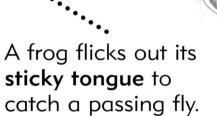

A frog flicks out its **sticky tongue** to catch a passing fly.

Sticky **pads** on a frog's fingers and toes stick tightly to a branch or a leaf.

When a frog calls out to other frogs, it puffs out its throat like a balloon and makes a loud croaking noise.

Jaguar

The jaguar is the biggest and most powerful cat in the rain forest. It can climb trees and swim after crocodiles. At night, the jaguar prowls the forest floor alone. Then it lies in wait for animals to eat. During the day, it relaxes in a tree or patch of grass.

Long **whisker** help a jaguar feel its way through the thick grass.

Playing is a fun way for a young **cub** to learn how to fight and hunt.

A jaguar is a fierce hunter. When hungry, it creeps up on an animal. Suddenly, it pounces before the animal can escape.

A spotted **coat** makes a jaguar hard to see in the shady grass and trees.

It's comfortable up here! A tree is a perfect place to lie in wait for a tasty meal or to take an afternoon nap.

Soft padded **paws** hide a jaguar's dangerous, sharp claws.

Snake

Snakes slither across the dark forest floor and climb trees. The emerald tree boa in the big picture is hanging from a branch, ready to pounce on a tasty frog snack. After a really big meal, it may not eat again for a year!

This viper is about to attack. It will dart forward, then sink its fangs into its enemy.

A snake **coils** its body tightly around a branch to keep steady.

As a snake moves along, rough **scales** help it grip the slippery branches. The colors on this snake's scales make it hard to see among the leaves.

Poison flows through the **fangs** of some snakes.

A snake's **jaw** stretches wide to swallow animals whole.

You smell food with your nose, but a snake smells with its **forked tongue!**

19

Crocodile

A crocodile spends the day lying lazily in the warm sunshine. In the evening, it floats silently in a cool river, keeping its eyes just above the water, on the lookout for its next meal.

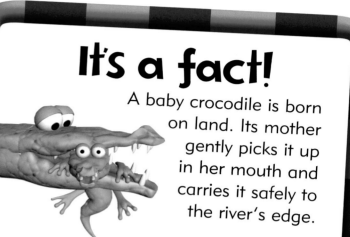

It's a fact!

A baby crocodile is born on land. Its mother gently picks it up in her mouth and carries it safely to the river's edge.

When a crocodile dives, its **nostrils** shut tight to stop water from flowing in.

A crocodile's sharp **teeth** and strong jaws are perfect for snapping up tasty fish and even large animals.

A crocodile swims by swishing its long, **powerful tail** from side to side.

A crocodile waddles along the ground on short, **stocky legs**.

Webbed feet make it easier to walk on soft, muddy ground.

This crafty crocodile looks like a floating log covered in weeds. But watch out — with one swish of its tail, it will pounce!

Insects and spiders

There are more insects in the rain forest than any other animal. An insect has six legs and three main parts to its body, which has a tough covering. A spider has eight legs. It has fangs and can spin silk. Spiders feed mostly on insects!

A **leafcutter ant** carries part of a leaf back to its nest to make food.

This shiny beetle hides among the leaves of plants, or burrows into woody stems, where it is safe from attackers.

A hard **case** protects the ant's body like a tough coat of armor.

A **butterfly** lands on a leaf to drink the sweet juice from a nearby flower.

Most butterflies have wings with beautiful **patterns**.

A butterfly's tongue is a long, hollow **tube**. It sucks up juice like a straw.

It's a fact!

There's a bird-eating spider that can grow as big as a dinner plate!

An ant smells, tastes, and touches the world around it with **feelers**. Most insects have feelers.

The forest floor

On the dark, damp forest floor, all kinds of animals are busy hunting, playing, and looking after their families.

How is the crocodile carrying its baby to the water?

Words you know

Here are words that you read earlier in this book. Say them out loud, then find the things in the picture.

webbed feet	paws	feelers
forked tongue	cubs	pads

How many ants are crawling along the log?

What is the red and yellow butterfly drinking?

Did you know?

The jaguar symbolized strength and courage to the ancient Maya Indians. They considered the animal a god.

There are only about 15,000 jaguars left in the wild.

A group of monkeys is called a "troop."

Hummingbirds can fly backwards.

More bats live in the rain forests of tropical America than anywhere else.

Bats are the only mammals that can fly.

Scientists believe that more than 50 wild species of plants and animals become extinct every day because of rain forest destruction.

Puzzles

Close-up!

We've zoomed in on parts of some animals' bodies. Can you figure out which animals you are looking at?

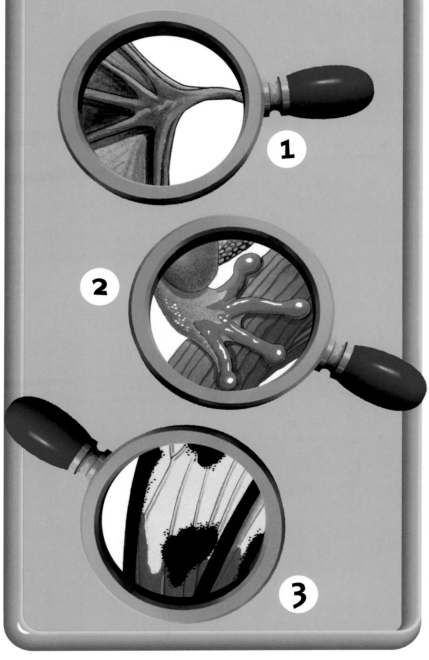

1

2

3

Follow me!

Can you figure out where the macaw, crocodile, and jaguar live in the rain forest? Follow the lines to find out!

macaw   crocodile   jaguar

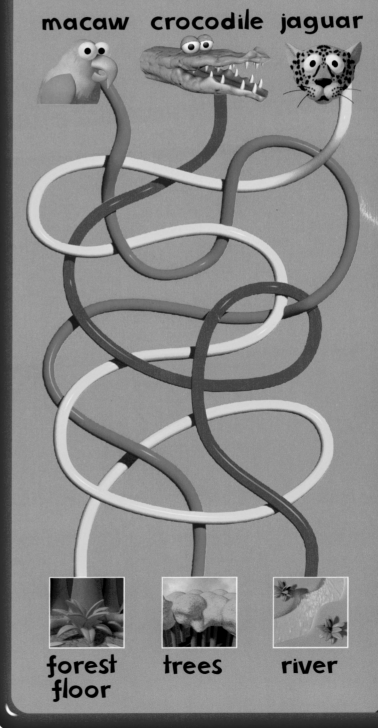

forest floor   trees   river

Answers on page 32.

Match up!

Match each word on the left with its picture on the right.

1. bat

2. sloth

3. hummingbird

4. jaguar

5. frog

6. ant

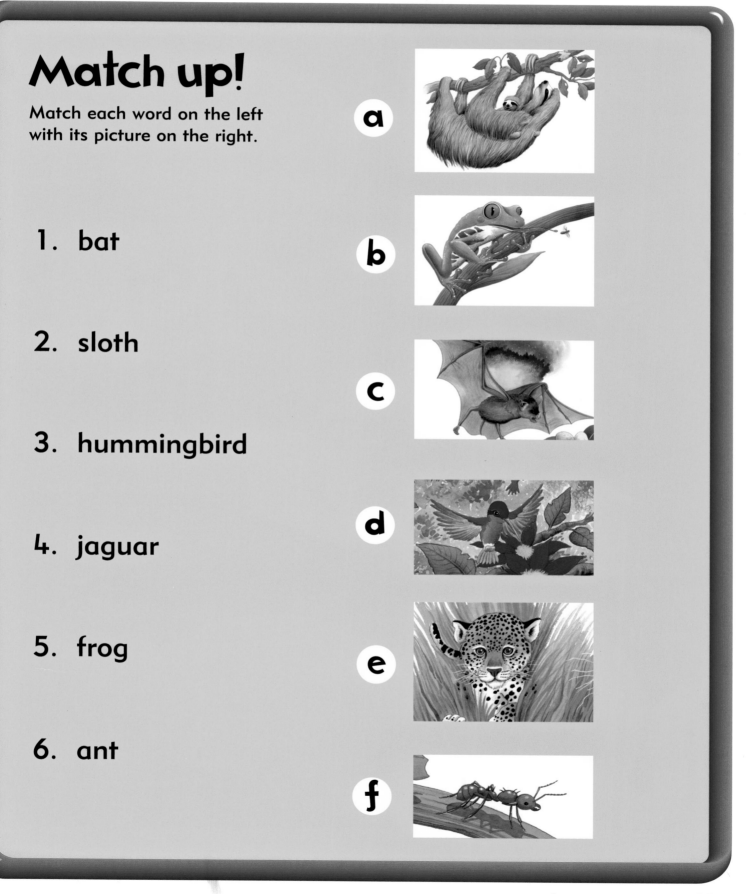

Answers on page 32.

True or false

Can you figure out which animals are telling the truth? You can go to the page numbers listed to help you find out the answers.

A bird-eating spider can be as big as a table. **Go to page 23.**

3

A howler monkey never makes noise. **Go to page 5.**

1

A mother crocodile carries her babies in her mouth. **Go to page 20.**

4

2

When a baby snake hatches, it bites a hole in its egg with a special tooth. **Go to page 19.**

The smallest hummingbird could perch on the end of a pencil. **Go to page 10.**

5

Answers on page 32.

Find out more

Books

Animal Babies in Rain Forests, Jennifer Schofield (Kingfisher, 2004)
By the babies you will know the parents and learn what life in a rain forest is like for both generations.

Fabulous Fluttering Tropical Butterflies, Dorothy Hinshaw Patent (Walker & Company, 2003)
This book helps you see that butterflies are some of the most colorful creatures in the rain forest and that their colors help them survive.

Jungle, Theresa Greenaway (Dorling Kindersley Publishing, 2004)
Romp through these pages and discover the beauty and strangeness of the world's jungles.

The Living Rain Forest: An Animal Alphabet, Paul Kratter (Charlesbridge Publishing, 2004)
Each letter of the alphabet introduces a different rain forest animal, from the anteater to the zorro.

Rain Forest Animals, Helen Frost and others (Capstone Press, 2002) 10 volumes
Each volume features one of these ten animals: boa constrictor, chimpanzee, gorilla, jaguar, leaf-cutting ant, lemur, parrot, tarantula, tiger, and tree frog.

Websites

Amazon Animals, Jungle Photos
http://www.junglephotos.com/amazon/amanimals/amanimals.shtml
Click on one of six groupings—mammals, reptiles, amphibians, birds, fish, and invertebrates—for photos of the animals in each group.

Habitats . . . Rain Forest, O. Orkin Insect Zoo
http://www.insectzoo.msstate.edu/OrkinZoo/rainForest.html
Of special interest to kids are the three sound files that have recorded sounds of insects living in the forest.

Rain Forest at Night, National Geographic
http://www.nationalgeographic.com/earthpulse/rainforest/index_flash.html
Scan your mouse over one of two darkened screens, one of the forest floor and one of the upper layer, to reveal an animal that is active at night.

Rainforest Animals, The Animal Network
http://www.rainforestanimals.net
Choose from a list of animals to open a screen that displays photos of the animal, a map showing where it lives, and facts about its behavior.

Tropical Rainforest Cluster, Science Museum of Minnesota
http://www.thinkingfountain.org/nav/tropicalcluster.html
Press the "Strata" button and explore the different levels of a rain forest from the ground to the treetops to find the animals that live in each.

Answers

Puzzles
from pages 28 and 29

Close-up!
1. bat
2. frog
3. butterfly

Match up!
1. c
2. a
3. d
4. e
5. b
6. f

True or false
from page 30

1. false
2. true
3. false
4. true
5. true

Index